THE OLD CLOAK

'Seeking God's Power of Old in Today's Church; Understanding the Sacredness of Christian Discipleship'
[2 Kings 2:1-18.]

APOSTLES DAVID E. & MARIE E. BUMTJE

<u>PREFACE</u>.

In this testimony, I try to briefly share the grace of Jehovah for some of us concerning the Old Cloak. As a pastor under pastors usually called elders in thousands of committed members and with a high standard of discipleship, living by example with a life of reading and meditation of Jehovah's word, fasting and prayers, evangelism on making disciples not talking about giving. All the things I mentioned above were done with great zeal. We were taught, and we taught how Yahweh gave all, but unfortunately, we were giving gradually. Once someone enters full-time in ministry under the congregation, he quits his job but keeps his belongings. He receives a monthly salary whether serving locally or sent oversea. I was so engaged as I was giving a zone to win souls for Christ as it was common in the congregation. Before joining this congregation, I asked Yahweh if I was to serve Him full-time or both, and He told me both. I was reluctant to enter this type of full-time with a salary until one day, Yahweh, who brought me into this great congregation spoke to me that it was time to leave the congregation to serve Him full-time with hundred percent surrender like the apostles of old in the book of **Acts 2:44-47** and **Acts 4:34-36.** I went to the extent of giving up even all my clothes and were given few cloths from the altar from others who had also surrendered. Then Jehovah asked all of us to make doo the Nazarite vow according to **Numbers: 6** and entered into a covenant with Him. In this closet, Yahweh, like with the Israelites on Mount Sinai, was spelling out His part of the covenant and ours. Like Abraham, one Friday night, under the leadership of apostle Bate Tataw Mercy Beyang, Yahweh ordered my wife and i to leave our homeland the following day to a foreign land we have never been, we knew not the road, we knew nobody; we tried to ask for few days like Monday, the Lord insisted, and we obeyed. The Old Cloak. Prior to this night, He told us that we were to go out of the country without mentioning it. So, He provided us money for our passports many months before this great night. Beloved, I am not going to write all this great testimony, but I am trying to encourage us through this ministry of literature Yahweh has entrusted into the hands of some of us that it is not in vain Yahweh calls us His chosen people as He told the Israelite that He was the Portion of the Levites, the manifestation of His promise and the release of His grace did not cancel the implementation of the Old Cloak. For years we have been under this Old Cloak of His grace with an orphanage to take care but never have we found ourselves in lack though not in the television; we witness The Jehovah of old with the same footsteps as it was in the very beginning. In fact, Yahweh prohibited apostle Mercy from opening even a website for pledges on behave of the orphanage

But ye are a chosen generation, a royal priesthood, a holy nation, a peculiar people; that ye should show forth the praises of him who hath called you out of darkness into his marvelous light; Which in time past were not a people, but are now the people of God: which had not obtained mercy, but now have obtained mercy. Dearly beloved, I beseech you as strangers and pilgrims, abstain from fleshly lusts, which war against the soul; 1 Peter 2:9-11.

MISSIONARIES
APOSTLES DAVID E. & MARIE E. BUMTJE

Unless otherwise indicated, all Scripture quotations are taken from the King James Version of the Bible.

THE OLD CLOAK

TABLE OF CONTENTS

INTRODUCTION

When supposed New Testament teachings propose that today's Christian has nothing to do with the law--especially the old testament's happenings-- taking Pentecost and the Holy Spirit's permanent residence in such a Christian as the reason, it seems they've missed a line of truth.

Besides, you may wonder if they've simply cut out the acts of the Old Testament alongside the fact that everyone who had the privilege of relationship with God in the past only did, through God's Spirit. Hence, questions should arise in our hearts--as disciples-- about the substantial presence of God's power, works, and Spirit in the old times and how the same can't be exactly said about today's church.

It should be troubling that though today's Christians possess the Holy Spirit in their inward parts, the power of God seems vague or absent. Yes, shouldn't this bother today's Christian? You should ask, "where is the power and that presence of God's Spirit; the same power that the prophets of old desired and sought after but was reserved for us according to 1 Peter 1:10-12?"

Without a doubt, whether the Old Testament or the church of Christ that was born on Pentecost, the power and presence of God remains constant. However, there's no contention as to the acceptable and only way to fellowship with God--belief in Jesus Christ. Yet, there seems to be an evident disconnection or falling away in today's church concerning God's power and Spirit.

Several thoughts may run through your mind as to why this is the case with today's Christians. The scriptures describe that the church is built upon the foundations of the prophets and apostles--meaning the Old Testament and New Testament-- with Christ as its cornerstone. More so, taking Abraham--the first to be saved through faith- as an example, you'd realize that the Eternal God dealt with Abraham and called him a friend.

Indeed, their relationship felt like two intimate friends sitting around the table for a good round of discussion. More so, the same is evident between Christ and His disciples--He called them friends, too. But it appears that perhaps our assessment, judgment, and understanding often leads us to ignore or neglect these signs of the Church's foundation--and this couldn't be God's will.

God's will should be carried out and facilitated by His Spirit in every Christians today. Compare the days of Joseph--when no stone tablets existed--yet a teenager--Joseph-- who was sold into an idolatrous nation still kept the commandments of Jehovah. Surely, this was because God's Spirit influenced his discipline and reverence for God.

Likewise, shouldn't today's Christians cling to the grace supplied by God's Spirit--to be like Joseph-- so the power and presence of God in their lives will be evident? In contrast, we seem to have the Holy Spirit, yet we lack discipline; we seem to lack the fear of Jehovah; perhaps our mind is focused on bread.

Expressly, our topic--the Old Cloak-- will center on the book of 2 Kings 2:1-18. There's Elisha--Elijah's disciple-- who asked to inherit the double portion of God's anointing upon his master. And I perceive that it's similar to Christ's promise to His disciples--today's Christians-- in John 14:12(KJV), *"Verily, verily, I say unto you, He that believeth on me, the works that I do shall he do also; and greater works than these shall he do; because I go unto my Father."*

It seems a reminder of the above is needed to inject today's church and Christians with a yearning and desire for God's power and presence. Indeed, the Old Cloak should depict or interpret the desire for God's power in today's Christian world, just as it was in old times. This book is to stir today's Christian to seek after the lord's power, Spirit, and presence--both in their lives and that of others.

This book will explore God's will for today's Christians--His disciples-- by taking a glance at His ways of operation in the Old Testament--of course, through the lenses of Christ. Besides, it's clear that all scripture is given for our benefit, and no part of it should be neglected or ignored because of the seepage of erroneous teachings that proposes the Old Testament to be archaic and useless for today's Christian.

Hence, we'll explore God's old ways--in the light of Christ-- to inspire a revival in our lives; lukewarmness in today's church must be done away with by God's power. I enjoin you today, follow me on this journey; let's secure the Old Cloak!

CHAPTER ONE

THE CHURCH; GOD'S FAMILY SYSTEM

"And I will make thy seed as the dust of the earth: so that if a man can number the dust of the earth, then shall thy seed also be numbered."

\- Genesis 13:16(KJV)

\-

It was to Abraham that the promise of a seed was given, a seed that will eventually birth many nations--Christians, God's family. However, in Galatians, Paul established that those who claim to be Abraham's descendants by flesh aren't true descendants of Abraham. Furthermore, he explained that except you worship and have a relationship with God through faith in Christ—Abraham's seed--

you're not part of God's family--Abraham's descendants.

Hence, the basis and foundation of the Christian faith--Old or New Testament-- is belief in Christ, just as Galatians 3:6-7 puts it, *"Even as Abraham believed God, and it was accounted to him for righteousness. Know ye therefore that they which are of faith, the same are the children of Abraham."*

Evidence that the Old Testament patriarchs are equal beneficiaries of God's grace is seen in Hebrews Chapter eleven--the topic of faith. Indeed, Hebrews discusses the acts of the Old Testament saints as an example to today's Christians. However, today's Christians standout specifically due to the permanent residence of the Spirit in them while yet in this present world--anyone who doesn't have the Spirit of Christ is none of His. Likewise, the Old Testament Christians worshipped God acceptably, too--for their dispensation-- via the residence of God's Spirit in the temple--the Ark of the Covenant and the light that never went out in the Holy of Holies.

Every family has a trait, a peculiar character that stands them out always. Likewise, God's family--the Church--reflects His character. More so, God's family--the church-- isn't a building or a place, but a people knitted together in God's love--in fellowship with the Holy Spirit. Hence, as a Christian, you should emulate the firstborn of God's family--Christ. Hence, regardless of who you were before you became a Christian--entered into God's fold--it's time to look to the Father's template to understand how His family operates.

Indeed, operation in God's family can't be better revealed anyway or anywhere else than in the Scriptures--the divinely and rightly interpreted scriptures. And today's Church seems to have its work cut out in this aspect. Meanwhile, the scriptures and laws of Moses were read in the synagogues--publicly and regularly-- in the days of Ezra. Thus, they enjoyed the outpouring of God's word. Similarly, today's Church should study, listen, and follow God's word in reverence and awe. Indeed, this is how to display your character and birthright as God's child.

Nevertheless, the Spirit of Christ is the ultimate seal and evidence that God's your Father and you're His child. And it's high time you knew that only Christ made this possible, according to Ephesians 3:15, *"Of whom the whole family in heaven and earth is named,"* But do you wonder how God's family operates, or what purpose to fulfill as a member of His family?

GOD'S FAMILY SYSTEM

"Now, therefore, ye are no more strangers and foreigners, but fellow citizens with the saints, and of the household of God;"

- Ephesians 2:19(KJV)

-

Theologian Wayne Grudem defines the church as "the community of all true believers of all time." He added that the Church "must equally include the true believers of all time—both those of the New Testament and those of the Old Testament age." Hence, his submission bears a striking resemblance with the letter of

Paul to the Ephesians. Ephesians also discusses the church as God's family and Christ's body.

But when you study the scriptures, you'd understand God's template, and the Church's role is also revealed. Hence, within God's family, saints—human beings—can only assume one prominent position, and it's the role of God's children. As children of God, you're loved with God's everlasting love, and God has no favorites, according to Romans 2:10-11, *"But glory, honor, and peace, to every man that worketh good, to the Jew first, and also to the Gentile: For there is no respect of persons with God."* More so, according to Deuteronomy 10:17, *"For the LORD your God is God of gods, and Lord of lords, a great God, a mighty, and a terrible, which regardeth not persons, nor taketh reward:"*

Hence, all Christians are equally grafted into every promise and blessing that God gives His children in His word. Indeed, in the family of God, today's Christians and those of the Old Testament are all born and adopted through the sacrifice that Jesus made on the cross—to save the human race—and the work that the Spirit does in each of them.

Subsequently, God's family are united in faith concerning the Lordship of Christ and His salvation because Romans 1:17 says, *"For therein is the righteousness of God revealed from faith to faith: as it is written, The just shall live by faith."* Again, the Apostle John affirms something quite similar, in the first chapter of John; John 1:12-13, *"But as many as received him, to them gave he power to become the sons of God, even to them that believe on his name: Which were born, not of blood, nor of the will of the flesh, nor of the will of man, but of God."*

So you'd realize the set up in God's family and how it depends on faith in God's Son—Christ Jesus. Without a doubt, through Him, you have the right to be children of God. More so, this whole procession is described as the new birth—spiritual—because it's not by human will but by God's divine and powerful will. Hence, God designed His family so all who are reborn and regenerate will be part of it.

Furthermore, the implications of the new birth are imminent in the reality of spiritual adoption, according to Romans 8:15, *"For ye have not received the spirit of bondage again to fear; but ye have received the Spirit of adoption, whereby we cry, Abba, Father."* This implies that you're equally adopted by God into His family system.

Pastor John MacArthur says, "Adoption is the act of incorporating a person who has been begotten by another person into one's own family." Since by default, non-regenerated people are considered to be Satan's descendants, the only way to become God's child is through spiritual adoption, as Paul writes in Galatians 4:4-5, *"But when the fulness of the time was come, God sent forth his Son, made of a woman, made under the law, to redeem them that were under the law, that we might receive the adoption of sons."*

If you understand the above, what questions should pop up in you; what's your purpose as God's child? Why does God have a family system? What's the Church's mandate, and how much is today's Church obedient to such mandate?

GOD'S CHURCH, THE CONDUIT

A conduit is a narrow channel or passage of personal communication. Who does God communicate through; who's God's channel or passage? Will God send any representative who doesn't belong to Him in a world of diverse identities? According to Paul in 2 Corinthians 5:20, *"Now then we are ambassadors for Christ, as though God did beseech you by us: we pray you in Christ's stead, be ye reconciled to God."*

Are you indeed an ambassador for Christ? Are you a conduit? Romans 10:14-15 says, *"How then shall they call on him in whom they have not believed? And how shall they believe in him of whom they have not heard? And how shall they hear without a preacher? And how shall they preach, except they be sent? As it is written, How beautiful are the feet of them that preach the gospel of peace, and bring glad tidings of good things!"*

Moreover, the Church has operated as God's conduit since the Old Testament, according to Luke 16:29, *"Abraham saith unto him, They have Moses and the prophets; let them hear them."* More so, Hebrews 1:1 says, *"God, who at sundry times and in divers manners spake in time past unto the fathers by the prophets,"* So since ages past, God made the Church—through the prophets—a channel of His message.

Likewise, God's message continued to be proclaimed until His message—Christ—appeared in the flesh, according to John 1:14, *"And the Word was made flesh, and dwelt among us, (and we beheld his glory, the glory as of the only begotten of the Father,) full of grace and truth."* Hence, His message—Christ—likewise prepared His disciples—the Church—by giving them the right to be God's conduit when He left the world.

Without a doubt, what Christ told His disciples confirmed their statuses as God's conduit—Mark 16:15-16, *"And he said unto them, Go ye into all the world, and preach the gospel to every creature. He that believeth and is baptized shall be saved, but he that believeth not shall be damned."*

"Go into all the world and preach the gospel", Jesus commands you. Indeed, today's church should perk up in this area—you may be too comfortable to keep your faith in yourself, whereas the Lord expects otherwise. Hence, unless you fulfill this charge or command, your place as a conduit may be compromised. Similarly, today's church should realize that their ultimate mandate is to be a soul-winning and soul-seeking enterprise—the gospel must be preached with great intent.

If the predisposition of today's church is similar to that of Prophet Jeremiah, it must also end at Jeremiah's resolve in Jeremiah 20:8-9, *"For since I spake, I cried out, I cried violence and spoil; because the word of the LORD was made a reproach unto me, and a derision, daily. Then I said, I will not make mention of him, nor speak any more in his name. But his word was in mine heart as a burning fire shut up in my bones, and I was weary with forbearing, and I could not stay."*

More so, the church should emulate Paul's commitment in 1 Corinthians 9:16, *"For though I preach the gospel, I have nothing to glory of for necessity is laid upon me; yea, woe is unto me, if I preach not the gospel!"* Be encouraged and stirred to become God's true conduit via witnessing the gospel today. Indeed, to be a conduit or heaven's ambassador may be hectic. Yet, today's church should value the importance of God's intention—to bring humans to God for salvation and transformation, to turn them into new creations. Finally, Christ discusses the tools He has provided for this work in Mark 16:17-18, *"And these signs shall follow them that believe; In my name shall they cast out devils; they shall speak with new tongues; they shall take up serpents; and if they drink any deadly thing, it shall not hurt them; they shall lay hands on the sick, and they shall recover."* Without a doubt, these are signs of God's power among His church. When today's Church becomes conduits—to bring new souls, His power to save those souls will be on display. But more glaringly, you'd realize that you're a conduit because God yearns to become the Father of many, just as He's yours.

GOD'S FATHERHOOD TO HIS CHILDREN

"God having provided some better thing for us, that they without us should not be made perfect."

-Hebrews 11:40(KJV)

Many times, you may tend to think that only the New Testament Church is entitled to the benefits that accompany God's fatherhood. Meanwhile, God shares His nature as Father towards the saints of old, too. But why is the fatherhood of God towards both Old and New Testament Christians so vaguely believed or discussed in today's Church--alongside its beneficial examples to the present Church? Moreover, didn't Paul write that many things that occurred in the Old Testament are written for our examples? Likewise, today's Christians should be beneficiaries of the Old

Testament's acts and saints. According to 2 Timothy 3:16-17, *"All scripture is given by inspiration of God, and is profitable for doctrine, for reproof, for correction, for instruction in righteousness: That the man of God may be perfect, thoroughly furnished unto all good works."*

But why did the Pharisees find the words of Jesus, when He referred to God as Father, to be blasphemous?

Without a doubt, until Christ surfaced, several facets or perspectives about God were rampant. The fathers of old referred to Him in different ways--El Shaddai, Adonai, Jehovah Jireh, Jehovah Rapha, Jehovah Nissi, Jehovah Makadesh-- but never referred to God as a father.

More so, during the dispensation of the Old Testament, many believed that whoever saw God physically would die. Likewise, the Pharisees of Jesus' time believed that God gave birth to no one--so they considered it blasphemous when He called God His Father. But this seemed different from Isaiah's prophecy in Isaiah 7:14, *"Therefore the Lord himself shall give you a sign; Behold, a virgin shall conceive, and bear a son, and shall call his name Immanuel."*

Indeed, Immanuel interprets--God with us. This is sufficient to put the claims of the Pharisaical belief system to bed because Christ, the only begotten Son of God, was sent into the world. More so, you'd realize that Christ, God's Son, the only one who had seen God, was sent into this world to show us the way to the Father.

Hence, John 1:14 says, *"And the Word was made flesh, and dwelt among us, (and we beheld his glory, the glory as of the only begotten of the Father,) full of grace and truth."* Clearly, the Pharisees didn't realize that their religious claims had been defeated. Instead, they had a hard time wrestling with the fact that God had a son who He sent in human flesh to procure salvation to the human race.

Nonetheless, the prophets of old were not in the dark. According to Hebrews 1:1, *"God, who at sundry times and in divers manners spake in time past unto the fathers by the prophets,"* Again, prophet Isaiah said these words in Isaiah

9:6, *"For unto us a child is born, unto us a son is given: and the government shall be upon his shoulder: and his name shall be called Wonderful, Counsellor, The mighty God, The everlasting Father, The Prince of Peace."* So, isn't it obvious that the Pharisees would have done better to study the scripture to find out that God prophesied the coming of His Son?

Today, are you like the Pharisees and Sadducees, too? Do you spread heresies that are unfounded in scriptures--that God's no father of His children; that those of the Old Testament aren't partakers in the gift of the Son of God? Don't you realize that the same Spirit at work during the Old Testament is also at work in these times; and that Christ is the same yesterday, today, and forever?

Nevertheless, God's fatherhood to His children in the Old Testament is clear, let's see what God told Moses in Exodus 4:22-23, *"And thou shalt say unto Pharaoh, Thus saith the LORD, Israel is my son, even my firstborn: And I say unto thee, Let my son go, that he may serve me: and if thou refuse to let him go, behold, I will slay thy son, even thy firstborn."* Dear

Christian, does this scripture clear your doubts? Do you see that God referred to the fathers of old as His son?

However, is the sonship of today's Christian under threat? Oh, no, but according to Romans 8:16-17, *"The Spirit itself beareth witness with our spirit, that we are the children of God: And if children, then heirs; heirs of God, and joint-heirs with Christ; if so be that we suffer with him, that we may be also glorified together."*

Hence, you should realize that God's fatherhood extends to the saints of old who believed in the coming of God's Son--Christ Jesus-- as much as the Christians of the New Testament did. Subsequently, Stephen said in Acts 3:22-23, *"For Moses truly said unto the fathers, A prophet shall the Lord your God raise up unto you of your brethren, like unto me; him shall ye hear in all things whatsoever he shall say unto you. And it shall come to pass, that every soul, which will not hear that prophet, shall be destroyed from among the people."*

Stephen spoke these words in a bid to convince the Pharisees and Sadducees that Christ was that prophet who Moses spoke about and the Son of God, too. Therefore, he explained that only obedience to Christ was required for God to be their Father.

Finally, you'd realize that both they, of Old, and we of the New Testament are joint heirs, through Christ our Lord. Hebrews 11:39-40 says, *"And these all, having obtained a good report through faith, received not the promise: God having provided some better thing for us, that they without us should not be made perfect."* In this scripture, the concept of all Christians' joint heritage--Old or New Testament—is established— and indeed, God is the Father of all Christians.

While this is true, why does today's Church seem to lack the power that their Old Testament counterparts enjoyed? Why does the Church seem to play second fiddle when it comes to fear and reverence for God? Didn't Paul warn Christians not to take the grace of God in vain, and didn't Jude equally complain that many take God's grace as a reason to be licentious?

Likewise, where are the manifestations of God's undiluted power in today's Church? Shouldn't the church take a clue from Elisha's request for a double portion of His master's anointing; isn't the church supposed to seek a revival of God's power and Spirit? If the fatherhood of God is evident upon today's Christians, why not cling to the words of the Lord in Luke 11:13, *"If ye then, being evil, know how to give good gifts unto your children: how much more shall your heavenly Father give the Holy Spirit to them that ask him?"*

CHAPTER TWO

THE CHRISTIAN'S PORTION; UNDERSTANDING ELISHA'S REQUEST FOR DOUBLE PORTION

"For whom he did foreknow, he also did predestinate to be conformed to the image of his Son, that he might be the firstborn among many brethren."

-Romans 8:29(KJV)

The term firstborn has two main meanings. The first is more literal, referring to the fact that this is the first son of a father. The second refers to the rights and authority of a person because they're the firstborn.

Meanwhile, the double portion is first mentioned in the Law of Moses in

Deuteronomy 21:17, *"But he shall acknowledge the son of the hated for the firstborn, by giving him a double portion of all that he hath: for he is the beginning of his strength; the right of the firstborn is his."*
Hence, every firstborn were entitled to twice the inheritance that was available to other children. Moreover, in ancient Israel, the firstborn child in every family was deemed special. Thus, the child was showered with several benefits. But the Hebrews did this, not only out of love or tradition but according to the set rules of God through Moses.
But more enlightening is the fact that among existing nations, peoples, tribes, and tongues, God decided to choose the nation of Israel--the Hebrews-- as His offspring, according to Exodus 4:22-23, *"Then you shall say to Pharaoh, 'Thus says the Lord: Israel is My son, My firstborn. So I say to you, "Let My son go that he may serve Me. But if you refuse to let him go, indeed, I will kill your firstborn."*
What does this imply in today's world? Similarly, Christ Jesus is the -firstborn- in all

ways and of all things. More so, God speaks expressly about His exalted position in Hebrews 1:5, *"For unto which of the angels said he at any time, Thou art my Son, this day have I begotten thee? And again, I will be to him a Father, and he shall be to me a Son?"* Furthermore, Christ has been appointed to have authority over all things, either in heaven, on earth, or under the earth, according to Philippians 2:9-10, *"Wherefore God also hath highly exalted him, and given him a name which is above every name: That at the name of Jesus every knee should bow, of things in heaven, and things in earth, and things under the earth;"*

Consequently, the firstborn only makes a rightful, due claim when He requests for inheritance from his father. With this clue, you can understand Elisha's request from Elijah, being his first disciple--firstborn of Elijah's prophetic ministry-- according to 2 Kings 2:9-10, *"And it came to pass, when they were gone over, that Elijah said unto Elisha, Ask what I shall do for thee, before I be taken away from thee. And Elisha said, I pray thee, let a double portion of thy spirit be upon me. And he said, Thou hast asked a hard thing: nevertheless, if thou see me when I am taken from thee, it shall be so unto thee; but if not, it shall not be so.*"

However, many people seem to misunderstand the meaning of Elisha's request for a double portion of Elijah's spirit. But in reality, Elisha was only asking for His rightful spiritual inheritance--and by nature, the firstling's portion is always a double portion.

Therefore, if Elijah typifies Christ--your ultimate Master-- and Christ represents God-- the Father-- while Israel represents today's Church--God's firstborn-- what's your best shot at God's double portion? On what conditions will such an inheritance apply?

Subsequently, in John 5:20, Christ says, *"For the Father loveth the Son, and sheweth him all things that himself doeth: and he will shew him greater works than these, that ye may marvel."*

Likewise, Christ said to His disciples in John 14:12, *"Verily, verily, I say unto you, He that believeth on me, the works that I do shall he do also; and greater works than these shall he do; because I go unto my Father."*

Hence, the same greater works--double portion-- that Christ received from His Father--being the Father's Son-- is promised to His disciples--today's Christians. This implies that Elisha's request is connected to Christ's promise of greater works to His disciples--believers.

More so, don't forget that the double portion simply implies the normal portion of the firstborn. Hence, Christ--God's firstborn-- has decided to share His inheritances with all Christians--His disciples. But as Elisha's inheritance depended on discipleship, today's Christians must undergo a similar prerequisite to be entitled to Christ's inheritance.

DISCIPLESHIP

Discipleship is the reality of loyally submitting to a certain master with who you share the same views. But more than this, discipleship may require unlearning and relearning at the master's feet. However, in Christianity, discipleship is the privilege of inheriting the Spirit of Christ; it's a spiritual matter. Hence, you'd realize that Elisha requested the double portion of Elijah's spirit instead of physical privileges.

Subsequently, there's no discipleship where the master's idea or spirit differs from the followers. Example is James and John in Luke 9:55, *"But he turned, and rebuked them, and said, Ye know not what manner of spirit ye are of."*

Nevertheless, it's established that the basic qualification for the double portion--the firstborn's inheritance-- is salvation and discipleship. Hence, without gainsaying, though Elisha was qualified on this basis, Elijah seemed to test His credentials as a worthy disciple further, according to 2 Kings 2:10, *"And he said, Thou hast asked a hard thing: nevertheless, if thou see me when I am taken from thee, it shall be so unto thee; but if not, it shall not be so."*

Similarly, though today's church should be encouraged by Elisha's resilience, they must shed off the minimum requirement mentality of salvation only. Subsequently, they must lay equal emphasis on the discipleship criteria too. But unfortunately, in today's Church, there seems to be a heretic dichotomy in the gospel of Christ.

Some preachers, in a bid not to be tough on their congregation, tend to erroneously dissociate the call to salvation from the call to discipleship. They seem to make the call to discipleship apply to only preachers, evangelists, teachers, and all other components of the five-fold ministry.

This can't be farther from the truth, don't be deceived! In contrast, Christ commands that all Christians must embark on preaching the gospel, according to Matthew 28:18-19, *"And Jesus came and spake unto them, saying, All power is given unto me in heaven and in earth. Go ye therefore, and teach all nations, baptizing them in the name of the Father, and of the Son, and of the Holy Ghost:"*

Besides, Christ further warned anyone who lacked the consistency to preach the gospel in Luke 14:28-30, *"For which of you, intending to build a tower, sitteth not down first, and counteth the cost, whether he have sufficient to finish it? Lest haply, after he hath laid the foundation, and is not able to finish it, all that behold it begin to mock him, Saying, This man began to build and was not able to finish."*

The double portion? Yes, it's for His dedicated disciples—true Christians. Wasn't Elisha resilient in strength and character despite every outward resistance? Likewise, didn't Christ's disciples of the early church experienced a similar fate when they knew that He was to be crucified?

According to John 16:19-20, *"Now Jesus knew that they were desirous to ask him, and said unto them, Do ye enquire among yourselves of that I said, A little while, and ye shall not see me: and again, a little while, and ye shall see me? Verily, verily, I say unto you, That ye shall weep and lament, but the world shall rejoice: and ye shall be sorrowful, but your sorrow shall be turned into joy."*

Without a doubt, the life of a true Christian--a disciple-- may not be a bed of roses. Indeed, you may be tempted to become stagnant or drawback from the Christian journey when difficult times surface. But true disciples follow in the step of their master. Certainly, the Holy Spirit has been given to assist all Christians to press on; and to develop the strength of character to push forward despite the obstacles. Isn't it beautiful to realize that Elisha's resilience proved efficient in the end? Though he was qualified--for the double portion— through Elijah's test, he understood that the reality of His inheritance was hinged on his reckless pursuit and loyalty to His master.

Likewise, the Christian's ultimate inheritance is the life everlasting that's embedded in the completion of their salvation at the end of this age. Moreover, Christ revealed His will for today's Church to remain resilient in Matthew 24:13, *"But he that shall endure unto the end, the same shall be saved."* Finally, you'd get to see the two sides of the same coin, to realize that salvation and discipleship activate the Christian's inheritance.

INHERITANCE

Inheritance means a permanent or valuable possession or blessing, especially one received by gift or without purchase; a benefaction. It's established that inheritance, similar to the definition of biblical grace, is a gift and not a reward. Hence, what's biblical inheritance--what's Christian inheritance?

Taking a clue from Elisha's request and eventual inheritance, did he request or receive a physical, material inheritance from His master? Subsequently, did you notice that their mode and terms of communication were spiritual? Now, is that how today's church perceives Christian inheritance?

Don't you wonder that while some preachers may propose material and physical blessings as your inheritance in Christ, the Scripture affirms that you were not born by the will of man, according to John 1:13, *"Which were born, not of blood, nor of the will of the flesh, nor of the will of man, but of God."*

Subsequently, if as a new creature—spiritual—you're qualified for Christian inheritance, why should you believe that the nature of your inheritance remains physical and material? In contrast, didn't Paul declare in Romans 14:17, *"For the kingdom of God is not meat and drink; but righteousness, and peace, and joy in the Holy Ghost."*

Indeed the baptism of the Holy Spirit is the foremost inheritance of the Christian, according to Ephesians 1:13-14, *"In whom ye also trusted, after that, ye heard the word of truth, the gospel of your salvation: in whom also after that ye believed, ye were sealed with that holy Spirit of promise, which is the earnest of our inheritance until the redemption of the purchased possession, unto the praise of his glory."*

Now, if Elisha's request can be described as the double portion of God's Spirit in Elijah, what was the implication of the inheritance upon Elisha? Can today's church connect this request and its implications to Jesus' words in Acts 1:8? *"But ye shall receive power, after that, the Holy Ghost is come upon you: and ye shall be witnesses unto me both in Jerusalem, and in all Judea, and in Samaria, and unto the uttermost part of the earth."*

More so, one of the functions of the Holy Spirit is to make you obedient, even till the end of this age--the second coming of Christ; the time for the completion of your salvation--according to Ephesians 4:30, *"And grieve not the holy Spirit of God, whereby ye are sealed unto the day of redemption."*

Likewise, the Holy Spirit reminds you that your true, everlasting inheritance--the adoption and complete redemption of your body--is yet to take place, according to Romans 8:23, *"And not only they, but ourselves also, which have the firstfruits of the Spirit, even we ourselves groan within ourselves, waiting for the adoption, to wit, the redemption of our body."*

Hence, shouldn't your eyes be fixed on the inheritance promised to today's Christians? Indeed, the Holy Spirit gives power to anyone who benefits from God's inheritance through Christ—by allocating His gifts and fruit--according to 1 Corinthians 12:4,7,11, *"Now there are diversities of gifts, but the same Spirit. But the manifestation of the Spirit is given to every man to profit withal. But all these worketh that one and the selfsame Spirit, dividing to every man severally as he will."* and according to Galatians 5:22-23 also, *"But the fruit of the Spirit is love, joy, peace, longsuffering, gentleness, goodness, faith, meekness, temperance: against such there is no law."*

Furthermore, Christ gives various descriptions of the Holy Spirit in the book of John--as a teacher, comforter, reminder, helper-- among others. He likewise emphasized the inheritance of power by His disciples according to Acts 1:8, *"But ye shall receive power, after that the Holy Ghost is come upon you:"* This is indeed similar to Elisha's exploits when he received the double portion of Elijah's anointing.

Hence, **He gave you the Holy Spirit to witness Him, using His power.** Notice that Elisha, after receiving His master's double portion, didn't embark on a different mission. Likewise, when you're given the Spirit of Christ, you're to continue His great works.

Indeed, Christ came to set men free from the hold of sin and death by offering everyone salvation. Hence, the evidence that you've obtained His inheritance is on display when you proclaim the gospel--of salvation for all men.

Without a doubt, you'd realize that the double portion handed down to you is a call to service, according to John 14:12, *"Verily, verily, I say unto you, He that believeth on me, the works that I do shall he do also; and greater works than these shall he do; because I go unto my Father."* This is the sign that you belong in God's household--His fold of Children--because Romans 8:9 says, *"But ye are not in the flesh, but in the Spirit, if so be that the Spirit of God dwells in you. Now, if any man has not the Spirit of Christ, he is none of his."*

Finally, **the Holy Spirit; God's mark of ownership; God's means of power; God's preservation until complete salvation;** your inheritance in this present world; the Spirit of Christ the Son of God, is the ultimate double portion that can validate and activate your soul, and that of today's Christians, as during old times.

CHAPTER THREE

THE PORTION; FATHER'S RICHES: HIS ANOINTING

"To an inheritance incorruptible, and undefiled, and that fadeth not away, reserved in heaven for you,"

-1 Peter 1:4(KJV)

As earlier said, perhaps today's Christians believe that their portions--as joint-heirs with Christ-- are the physical, material, are temporal pleasures that this world offers. But on the contrary, as Elisha accompanied Elijah long enough to realize that the most important wealth his master possessed was God's anointing, today's Christians must wake from their slumber to realize that the Father is Spirit, and for this reason, their true inheritance is spiritual.

Friend, there's a whole lot to your eternal inheritance. But what's most fascinating and min-blowing is that all Christians inherit God! According to the Old Testament, God was very specific about His people's inheritance. In those days, the Levites--Priests of the temple-- were not given a portion of Israel's land during allocation.

Instead, God said in Deuteronomy 18:1-2, *"The priests the Levites, and all the tribe of Levi, shall have no part or inheritance with Israel: they shall eat the offerings of the Lord made by fire, and his inheritance. Therefore shall they have no inheritance among their brethren: the Lord is their inheritance, as he hath said unto them."*

Though the priests got no land, they got something better; God! Furthermore, all Levites continued to serve the Lord in the tabernacle or temple, and they enjoyed the privilege of being separated from all mundane concerns because they had to focus on matters that pertained to the worship of God only.

Likewise, the New Testament makes a more glaring impression on what this implies for today's Christians. You'd notice that in 1 Peter 2:5, *"Ye also, as lively stones, are built up a spiritual house, an holy priesthood, to offer up spiritual sacrifices, acceptable to God by Jesus Christ."* Hence, being a priest of a Holy Priesthood, God Himself is your inheritance--your greatest possible treasure is God. **This means that you should rejoice in the hope of experiencing the fullness of God's glory one day!**

To emphasize God's glory--it's not the joy of seeing Grandma and Grandpa in eternity or to merely escape this present world and its prevalent affections, lusts, and desires. Instead, a true Christian reaffirms the psalmist's word, *"besides You, I desire nothing on earth."*

Likewise, Revelation 21:7 says, *"He that overcometh shall inherit all things; and I will be his God, and he shall be my son."* Besides, in the discourse about inheritance, **the Christian is entitled to facets of God's inheritances**--in this present world and beyond. This is why Paul announced in 1Corinthians 15:19 that, *"If in this life only we have hope in Christ, we are of all men most miserable."* Here, Paul communicated how real the inheritance of eternal life through Christ's resurrection was.

Another spectacular truth about your inheritance in Christ is that, while His death activated it, His eventual resurrection validated. So, in eternity, you inherit God and become an heir of His love, grace, and mercy; heirs of His faithfulness, truth, and righteousness; heirs of His wisdom, goodness, and power. **Indeed, all of God's attributes are directed towards you for good. Knowing this should spark a revival of joy in you and the drive to know Him in increasing measure.**

Let me query; is God is the treasure, the true inheritance? Are you a child of God? Has the Spirit testified with your spirit that you belong in His family? Do you have redefined affections and love towards God, and does the Holy Spirit enable you to cry out in intimacy with Him, saying, Abba Father?!

To dig deeper, Ephesians 1:3 says, *"Blessed be the God and Father of our Lord Jesus Christ, who hath blessed us with all spiritual blessings in heavenly places in Christ:"* What are these spiritual, heavenly blessings in Christ? It's established that they're far from the material, physical pleasures, but not far from spiritual realities like forgiveness of sins, holiness, justification, and adoption.

Subsequently, Jesus promised His followers-- you and I-- that the Holy Spirit will be sent to help. Hence, the Holy Spirit resides within and among all Christians, acting as the passport to living with Him in eternity, according to Ephesians 1:13-14, *"In whom ye also trusted, after that ye heard the word of truth, the gospel of your salvation: in whom also after that ye believed, ye were sealed with that holy Spirit of promise, Which is the earnest of our inheritance until the redemption of the purchased possession, unto the praise of his glory."*

Besides, according to 1 Corinthians 3:16, *"Know ye not that ye are the temple of God, and that the Spirit of God dwelleth in you?"* In the Old Testament, like Hannah, many found solace in the temple in towns of trouble, confusion, and especially King David, in the time of weakness. Hence, **if you're indeed the temple of the Holy Spirit, you're entitled to godly revelation, wisdom, and divine power.**

Furthermore, the Holy Spirit opens the believer's eyes to the hope of a true inheritance in Christ and helps sinners see the need for salvation--by convicting them. While in the business of salvation for sinners, Jesus knew that His disciples would need the power to carry out their mission as witnesses, so He gave them the Holy Spirit—power!

Consequently, when you bear witness about Christ to the world, there's a reward. This implies that whenever today's church puts the inheritance to work, make the benefit of being a Christian count; don't take the grace of God in vain; the Lord is pleased.

But in contrast, this doesn't seem to be the case with Christians who lose focus on the Lord's pleasure—they crave material and earthly things and become greedy—neglecting the

Master's pleasure. Therefore, I ask today, are your eyes fixed on the Ball--Christ and His pleasures-- according to the scriptures in Colossians 3:23-25? *"And whatsoever ye do, do it heartily, as to the Lord, and not unto men; Knowing that of the Lord ye shall receive the reward of the inheritance: for ye serve the Lord Christ. But he that doeth wrong shall receive for the wrong which he hath done: and there is no respect of persons."*

Do you work intently for the Lord's pleasure always? Are you making good use of the Lord's investment--inheritance-- in you? Indeed, this is no time to be greedy, earth-bound, and distracted from the heavenly course. Instead, be focused on eternity--that's how the Lord is pleased!

CHRISTIAN FOCUS; ETERNITY

"For our light affliction, which is but for a moment, worketh for us a far more exceeding and eternal weight of glory;"
-2 Corinthians 4:17(KJV)

As a Christian, the promise--the hope of communion with God forever-- should sustain you when faced with this world's trials. Indeed, the inheritance is promised to anyone who believes; it's reserved for those who hear the truth--about Jesus and receive the Holy Spirit; in short, for Christians only. Indeed, your Christian hope should lie resiliently in the fact that you'd lay hold on your portion; heritage, inheritance, and right, eventually.

John Calvin writes on inheritance, "We do not have the full enjoyment of it at present. Yet we walk in hope, and we do not see the thing as if it were present, but we see it by faith. Although, until then, the world gives itself liberty to trample us underfoot, as they say; although our Lord keeps us tried with many temptations; although he humbles us in such a way that it may seem we are as sheep appointed to the slaughter, so that we are continually at death's door, yet we are not destitute of a good remedy. And while seeing that the Holy Spirit reigns in our hearts, we have something for which to give praise even amid all our temptations. Therefore, we should rejoice, mourn, grieve, give thanks, be content, but wait"--from Calvin's Ephesians sermons, delivered in Geneva, 1558—59.

The Church is Christ's bride--your present and eternal heritage-- and whatever He inherits is extended to you. So as Christ is appointed heir over all things according--Matthew 28:18, *"And Jesus came and spake unto them, saying, All power is given unto me in heaven and in earth".* **"you're also entitled to proportions of the fullness of all things in Him--through inheritance".**

Besides, if your eyes are indeed fixed on Christ, the author and finisher of the Christian faith, His wonderful, eternal benefits will be showered on you. Don't forget that He told Pilate that His kingdom isn't of this world, so why don't you fix your gaze on Him and be guaranteed that you'd reign in His coming eternal kingdom?

More so, the Bible says that Christ inherits the world. Besides, God promises that you're an heir of this world also, as Jesus said in Matthew 5:5, *"Blessed are the meek: for they shall inherit the earth."* Here, you'd realize that your inheritance in this present world--Christ's fruit of meekness-- plays a role in your eternal inheritance.

Without a doubt, the earth and its works will be burned and ruined at the end of this age--to make place for God's new creation of a new heaven and earth-- where righteousness dwells. Hence, without a doubt, Christians would inherit this new world.

Imagine a world without sin, suffering, sickness, crying, pain, or death; with no armies, police, fire departments; a world where everyone prefers one another to themselves and seeks to serve others. Imagine a world without selfishness, or pride, or cruelty. Indeed, the bounties of eternity are numberless and beyond imagination, yet that's a clue of what you'd inherit!

Have you thought of God's promise of glorified Bodies, too? Now, you may bother and worry about sickness and infirmities of all sorts. Perhaps you may be publicly discredited for being ugly or unattractive. But all that matters eternally isn't what this world passes a remark on. Hence, many who are drifted from the course of the gospel into worldliness or those who won't give the gospel a chance are deceived.

But your inheritance in Christ certainly makes you qualified for an incorruptible, glorified body. Besides, the same way you bear Adam's likeness, now—spirit, soul, and body—Paul describes that you'd bear Christ's literal likeness, too--that flesh and blood can't inherit God's kingdom.

So, for Paul, to be glorified with Christ is to be raised in an incorruptible body, as written in 1 Corinthians 15:42-45, 47-50, *"So also is the resurrection of the dead. It is sown in corruption; it is raised in incorruption: It is sown in dishonor; it is raised in glory: it is sown in weakness; it is raised in power. It is sown a natural body; it is raised a spiritual body. There is a natural body, and there is a spiritual body. And so it is written, the first man Adam was made a living soul; the last Adam was made a quickening spirit. The first man is of the earth, earthy: the second man is the Lord from heaven. As is the earthy, such are they also that are earthy: and as is the heavenly, such are they also that are heavenly. And as we have borne the image of the earthy, we shall also bear the image of the heavenly. Now, this I say, brethren, that flesh and blood cannot inherit the kingdom of God; neither doth corruption inherits incorruption."*

If the Bible gives you such a clear hint about inheritance, what should your resolve be? When you understand and value the glory that awaits you, won't you be able to endure whatever trial comes your way? Knowing that you have God's guarantee, won't you praise God even during these trials? Indeed, 2 Corinthians 4:17 say, *"For our light affliction, which is but for a moment, worketh*

*for us a far more exceeding and eternal weight
of glory;"*

THE TRUE RICHES OF CHRIST

*"If therefore ye have not been faithful in the
unrighteous mammon, who will commit to your
trust the true riches?"*

-Luke 16:11(KJV)

A father once remarked, Son, when I leave this old earth, I won't be able to leave you much of this world's goods, but I'll leave you the whole world to make your living in. Isn't it only natural to desire sufficient resources to avoid poverty? But too many people seem to make the accumulation of earthly goods and personal wealth an all-consuming passion.

Hence, Lucretius remarked, But if one should guide his life by true principles, man's greatest riches is to live a life with a contented mind, for little is never lacking. Moreover, the scriptures better explain that the accumulation of earthly goods and riches, though pleasurable, isn't the primary goal of the Christian life.

The word—riches occurs many times in the Scriptures. Thus, Abram--Abraham-- was a wealthy man. But Proverbs 22:1 says, *"A good name is rather to be chosen than great riches, and loving favour rather than silver and gold."* Hence, though the Lord blessed Abraham abundantly, he was likewise rich in faith and became a household name because of his faith-- not his riches.

By itself, wealth may intoxicate the rich and make them proud, according to Jeremiah 9:23-24, *"Thus saith the LORD, Let not the wise man glory in his wisdom, neither let the mighty man glory in his might, let not the rich man glory in his riches: But let him that glorieth glory in this, that he understandeth and knoweth me, that I am the LORD which exercises lovingkindness, judgment, and righteousness, in the earth: for in these things I delight, saith the LORD."*

Likewise, Paul warned Timothy about anyone who considers the relationship with God-- godliness-- as a means to financial gain. Instead, Paul emphasized contentment in 1 Timothy 6:6-8, *"But godliness with contentment is great gain. For we brought nothing into this world, and it is certain we can carry nothing out. And having food and raiment let us be therewith content."*

Besides, Paul further warned that those who are greedy would fall into many traps and stumble--spiritually. Thus today's church may be culpable of the same error when they propagate the heresy that the Christian's inheritance is in how much earthly riches they've obtained. Perhaps the Church needs to follow Peter's advice to its leaders, according to 1 Peter 5:2, *"Feed the flock of God which is among you, taking the oversight thereof, not by constraint, but willingly; not for filthy lucre, but of a ready mind;"*

So, to know God through Christ and His redeeming work is to be rich indeed. The Scriptures speak expressly about the infinite riches of God--such riches that are beyond ephemeral. Consider Romans 9:23, *"And that he might make known the riches of his glory on the vessels of mercy, which he had afore prepared unto glory,"*

Without a doubt, God's mercy and glory are an aspect of His eternal riches. Indeed, God's mercy makes you worthy to enjoy eternity through Christ. Such mercy is eternal because He doesn't change His mind halfway into the reign of Christ--in the kingdom of His glory—that He's lost interest in your salvation. Hence, it's such reliable mercy that's always available for your inheritance.

Similarly, His riches of grace is beyond measure, according to Ephesians 1:7, *"In whom we have redemption through his blood, the forgiveness of sins, according to the riches of his grace;"* subsequently, another dimension of the same grace is defined in Ephesians 2:7, *"That in the ages to come he might shew the exceeding riches of his grace in his kindness toward us through Christ Jesus."*

More so, God gives strength to all Christians to do the work of ministry, and such strength is administered by His riches of grace also. Paul testified in Ephesians 3:8 saying, *"Unto me, who am less than the least of all saints, is this grace given, that I should preach among the Gentiles the unsearchable riches of Christ;"*

If Paul was endowed with God's grace to preach His unsearchable, numberless, unfathomable grace, how do you fare in the same aspect? In contrast, doesn't today's church seem to preach and teach heretical sermons that this world's material, temporal, and transient pleasures are God's seal of the Christian's inheritance--true riches?

Unfortunately, true riches--Christian inheritance-- doesn't comprise of material things, according to Jesus' temptation in Matthew 4:4, *"But he answered and said, It is written, Man shall not live by bread alone, but by every word that proceedeth out of the mouth of God."* Also, in Luke 12:15, *"And he said unto them, Take heed, and beware of covetousness: for a man's life consisteth not in the abundance of the things which he possesseth."*

Indeed, the scriptures further describe the riches of this world as uncertain riches. While uncertain riches can be accessed by carnal, ungodly, and natural human beings, true riches can't.

Hence, remember that's it's an unsearchable kind of riches--not unavailable to those who are God's children but to the world. Therefore, how can anyone access it or benefit from it? Can anyone without God's portion or inheritance get it? No! that's the hope of Christian inheritance.

CHAPTER FOUR

CONDITIONS FOR THE PORTION; BECOMING A TRUE CHRISTIAN

Right from the foundation of the Old Testament down to the zenith of the New Testament, God's Word remains a gold mine for the many promises of God. But one of the things I have realized is that these promises come with conditions that must be fulfilled to gain access to its realities. This simply means that God isn't obligated to keeping any of His promises to us if we don't meet His conditions first.

In the book of Second Kings 2, we read of Elijah's departure and how his servant: Elisha, followed him through despite the mockery of other sons of the prophets. Not only was Elisha challenged to go back by the sons of the prophets, but even Elijah also encouraged and advised him to stay back. But Elisha knew that it isn't by wonderful wishes that one step into God's power and the riches of God's wonderful presence.

Elisha stepped into power and relevance in His time because he fulfilled the condition of followership. The cloak that fell off from Elijah became the symbol of a double portion of Elijah's spirit. The sons of the prophets couldn't come into the possibilities of God's power, just like many Christians today, who are not ready to pay the price for God's power as of old.

I found three basic definitions of the word *'condition'* by the Merriam Webster's dictionary all-encompassing. First, it says, "condition is a premise upon which the fulfillment of an agreement depends."

Secondly, "a provision making the effect of a legal instrument contingent upon an uncertain something essential to the appearance or occurrence of something else. Also, it is "a restricting or modifying factor." Here, another word for the condition will be PREREQUISITE. What must you do to step into the inheritance God has for you as of Old?

In this chapter, we would discuss what it takes for today's Christians to inherit the cloak. Are there any qualifications, prerequisites, or necessities for the cloak's reception? Is there a degree of trust, faith, or consistency needed to be able to inherit God's supernatural power? Follow me through this chapter as I open you up to the conditions today's Christians must fulfill if they are ever going to receive the double portion of God's power.

HOW IMPORTANT ARE CONDITIONS IN SCRIPTURES TO ACCESSING ANY SPIRITUAL PROMISES OF GOD?

As free as the work of redemption is, have you ever seen any man who unconsciously became a Christian? Have you ever heard a genuine Christian say, "Oh, I never knew what I did to give myself to God? I just woke up a Christian?" How awkward would that sound if you found someone like that? I believe it would sound unbelievable, estranged from the teachings of scripture, and untrue. Salvation is free, but we have a part—confession and repentance—to come into its realities. God is committed to doing His part, but if you fail to do your part of the deal, the door into life will remain shut.

When you stumble on the promises of God with Abraham in the book of Genesis 12:2, you may think they were promises that come with no demands until you step back into verse one of the same chapter. God told Abraham to *"Get thee out of thy country, and from thy kindred, and from thy father's house, unto a land that I will show thee"* (Gen. 12:1). Abraham's success concerning becoming a great nation was dependent upon his meeting the conditions God had set. Not in the whirlpool of wishes in which many Christians are kept today. **We talk with much pride and arrogance about what God said without a corresponding heart of obedience to what God has commanded.**

Today's Christians must realize that God will never change His mode of operations because we have now come into the New Testament. Or because we now have the gift of the Holy Spirit after Pentecost. Have you ever wondered why many Christians walk through life powerless as though the streams of power that flowed ceaselessly in the times of Old has dried? The reason is very simple! The reason is that we seem to know too much on the head while our heart is little and not able to submit to God's dealings. Many are always quick to claim the Abrahamic covenant without stepping into the obedience of the Abrahamic patterns. God is never mocked; it is what we sow that we reap!

When Abraham fulfilled the condition of leaving his family, a generational lineage of God's power (the cloak) and multifaceted realities became opened to us—Christian. Consider a statement God made to Israel to prepare them for the promised land. He spoke through Moses, *"Behold, I set before you this day a blessing and a curse; A blessing, if ye obey the commandments of the Lord your God, which I command you this day: And a curse, if ye will not obey the commandments of the Lord your God..."* (Deut. 11:26-28).

The strength of God fulfilling that promise rests on that little two-letter word, "if"—it's a pointer to the conditions set upon their blessing. God's blessing over the called-out people of God (a symbol of the church) rests on their ability to do their part. The truth is, God's power doesn't come on lazy men. Even before the cloak of power could come on the disciples on the day of Pentecost, they had to fulfill certain critical conditions. Imagine they never took Jesus' words to stay at Jerusalem seriously. Would they have experienced the power of God as of old? Conditions are God's way of checking us out on how passionate and committed we are to Him. Power is not safe in the hand of a man that can't submit to its terms and conditions.

PREREQUISITES AND CONDITIONS FOR INHERITING GOD'S POWER

1. **Salvation:** The first condition that must be satisfied if you must be a true Christian (thereby worthy of God's inheritance) is that you believe in Jesus through faith for the salvation of your soul. Great power isn't just released to any random person, but to a person that has come into the provisions that have been made in Christ. This is why Paul revealed in Ephesians 2:8 that; *"For by grace are ye saved through faith; and that not of yourselves: it is the gift of God?"* (KJV)

If you would receive the portion of God's power, it's important you are first translated into the Kingdom of God. The bible says that **'Pearls are not to be cast before swine.'** Hence, everyone that will experience God's power must first come into His provisions by believing in Christ for the saving grace. Have you surrendered your life to Christ? Maybe you're even part of today's Christian who believes that one can carry God's power without accepting the Son of God—Jesus Christ.

The Apostles of Old knew this so much that they called the gospel the ***power of God.*** What a revelation they had of the power hidden in that first acceptance of the Son of God! When you think about Elisha in the Old Testament, you will see a man who came into the inheritance of Elijah's power even though he wasn't Elijah's biological son. We aren't Christ Jesus' biological sons, but we are adopted and received into the beloved because of the sacrifice He made. Just like Elisha came into the power of Old by following Elijah in Discipleship, we must be ready to follow Jesus without restraints.

The book of Luke 14:25-33 detailed how unreasonable it is to think you came to build a life that will withstand the storms of time and life without sitting down to count the cost. To follow Christ Jesus and house His power as of Old, you must be ready to fulfill some conditions. He highlighted them in the passage quoted above. Christ Jesus said If any man will come after Him—become a true Christian, what must he check first?

➤ First, what do I love more than Christ Jesus? Am I ready to put it aside and make Chris Jesus supreme? If not, you cannot walk in this power (even if you say you're a Christian).

➤ Secondly, are you ready to deny yourself? What are you ready to let go for Christ? If there's anything too big to let go for the sake of Christ, you're not worthy of this cloak. Can you see why we walk through life without the evidence of God's power now? Can you see why the power of God is becoming increasingly scarce in today's Christians?

➤ Thirdly, will you be ready to carry your cross (a symbol of shame and identification with Christ) and follow Him? If you have not ready to be identified with Christ, just like Elisha, never mind the shame he faced from the sons of the prophets; you're not worthy of the Old Cloak of Christ's power.

2. **Wait:** No one receives God's power in a rush! He's never in haste to commit Himself to men, but rather, He is very careful in delegating men that are unmade and uncut. He will not empower a man He has not trained; neither will He equip a man He does not prune! The book of Isaiah 40 is such a book that captures the flood of weaknesses and powerlessness that will sweep the world in the last days. *Now when he was in Jerusalem at the Passover, in the feast day, many believed in his name, when they saw the miracles which he did. But Jesus did not commit himself unto them, because he knew all men, John 2:23-24 KJV.*

See how the prophet captures the heart of God in bringing solutions to such a dilemma. *"Even the youths shall faint and be weary, and the young men shall utterly fall:* ***But they that wait upon the LORD shall renew their strength; they shall mount up with wings as eagles; they*** *shall run, and not be weary, and they shall walk, and not faint."* - Isaiah 40:30-31

The world system is designed to make the Christian faint and drained of strength. The only secret to God's power or the manifestation of His glory is **'waiting.'** You will never receive any power in God or from God if you don't wait patiently for it. Elisha was a servant who patiently waited on his master and served him. He wasn't a distant servant, and when Elijah was about to be taken away, he followed him everywhere, not minding the mockery he received from all angles. Power is only released to those who patiently wait on God! Think about Ruth. She waited patiently with her mother-in-law—Naomi—in discipleship before she could marry Boaz and bring life to a dying lineage. Do you want God's power as of Old? Are you ready to wait like the prophets, Apostles, and servants of Old?

3. **Obedience is a big deal:** A major strain to how people experience God's power is that they know too much that they cannot trust His instructions. God has not called you to

democracy or representative government. You're not supposed to debate His instructions or do selective perception about them. He wants you to just obey Him! Isn't that simple? Yes, it's that simple. You do not need to be smart, wise, or intelligent; you only need to be submissive to His counsel. *And now, Israel, what doth the Lord thy God require of thee, but to fear the Lord thy God, to walk in all his ways, and to love him, and to serve the Lord thy God with all thy heart and with all thy soul, Deuteronomy 10:12 KJV.*

God doesn't need you as a co-pilot to direct your life, and He wants you to be in the passenger's seat and trust Him to do the navigation. That's the power as of Old finds expression in a Christian. Joseph was such a man. He was in Egypt: a strange land where he had no family or friend, no one would have known if he had sinned or bowed to the sumptuous pressure of iniquity the devil offered. But then, he feared God and chose to obey His commandment. He obeyed God when there was no one around and took responsibility for it. Are you an obedient Christian? Many times, the devil will give you opportunities to sin against God. These sins will come with a promise of reward when no one is watching. **It's your ability to obey God that determines if He will ever trust you with His power.** When power is given to a dick, full of disobedience, he will use it to further his own course.

5. **Seek Him**: *"Evil men understand not judgment: but they that seek the LORD understand all things."* – Proverbs 28:5 (KJV). No man can possess God's power without having a deep understanding of who He is. He doesn't reveal His power first. He reveals Himself. If you don't seek to know God personally and you don't understand His ways, He can't trust you with His power. More so, seeking God requires conscious and deliberate effort or action. To know God, you must study His word and gain light through it. The word of the Lord makes wise, it enlightens, and it opens you up to instruction and spiritual information

that weakens the devil's intelligence systems. It's God's catalog on all life issues. If you ignore the power of God's word, you will lack a weapon to do spiritual warfare. There is something in it for all situations of your life. Furthermore, you have to dedicate yourself to prayer and supplications. Valuable things are not got without a price; hence, if you would have your God release His power on you, then it is pertinent to contend for it in the place of prayer.

GOD TESTING THE STRENGTH OF YOUR CONFIDENCE IN HIM

"Count it all joy, my brothers, when you meet trials of various kinds, for you know that the testing of your faith produces steadfastness. And let steadfastness have its full effect, that you may be perfect and complete, lacking in nothing."

- James 1:2-4 (ESV)

God does not want Christians who are only true to Him when things are working well. Today's Christians must come into the realm of nothing that can separate me from the love of God. Imagine the three Hebrew boys. They saw the power of God in the fire of life. I think gold glows more in the atmosphere of heat. Trials and temptations are opportunities for the seed of greatness in us to find expression. Men who will see the power of God must no count their lives worthy.

It was right in the midst of trials and fierce persecution that the early church rose in an unquenchable display of God's power and authority. To be a true Christian in a world that is hostile to your God, you must be ready to stand rigid and firm through the fire! We are in need of Christians in the fashion of Daniel today, who will not change their conviction because they heard the roaring of the lion. We wouldn't have known that God could still shut the mouth of lions if Daniel chickened out of trials for fear.

It's important you know that even when you fulfill the prerequisites listed above, God will deliberately test you to check the strength of your trust in Him. You see, every person in the bible who walked in God's power had been tried and proven before their manifestation. Joseph was trained through the prison, David was tried in the wilderness, and Jesus Christ was tried for forty days, but they all emerged from the tests as victors.

Finally, it's not God's method to commit Himself to a man that hasn't been tested, tried, and certified. Test always proceeds manifestation in God's formula. If you want the manifestation of God's power, you must have been put through the test and overcome. Are you ready to submit to God's pruning and making system—Discipleship—to bear the genuine power of God?

CHAPTER FIVE

NEW PORTION, NEW ORDERS?

"Remove not the ancient landmark, which thy fathers have set."

- Proverbs 22:8

One of the misconceptions that have hindered the flow of God's power through the ages is the mantra that Jesus came to do away with the ancient landmarks. Many believe that the coming of the Holy Spirit opened a new season to the church, and then the foundation on which the church was built for thousands of years before the dawn of the New Testament should be done away with. While we glory in the New Portion of the anointing, we completely neglect the fact that the New Portion never establishes a new order!

In fact, the glory and beauty of Christ Jesus' ministry shine in its full radiance when we see Him in His accurate relation to the Old Testament. We will see clearly what God is doing in the New Testament if only we give cognizance to the Old Order. This truth was adequately captured in the life of Elijah and Elisha, Moses and Joshua, Jesus and His disciples. I mean, when Elijah left the scene of ministry, he left Elisha a cloak (a representation of God's power—the portion). Did Elisha go ahead erect new orders or models of ministry or workings? NO! He understood that there's a flow that must be maintained with the Old cloak if the new portion must shine in its full color and brilliance.

When Elijah was about to be taken to heaven with a whirlwind, his cloak dropped from him and his student: Elisha picked it up immediately and started manifesting through it. As a matter of fact, his first miracle was done with the same Old Cloak. But wait, he asked for a double-portion anointing, for a power that was the multiple of his master's. when the cloak fell, he didn't just kneel down and continue crying to God, asking for his own cloak; s. Or asking for the cloak of Elijah to double in size, he instead teared down his own garment, took up the cloak and started manifesting in the strength of the Old Order.

The pain of today's Christian is that we love doing new things immediately. God release little graces and anointing on us. We quickly raise our shoulders with impunity and say, "well, God's doing a new thing now. So, forget about that old pattern of operations. It doesn't work anymore!" They completely forget that the Book of Romans revealed that Jesus (God manifest) is a constant being. He's the same yesterday, today, and forever. He doesn't change today because He's never confused about what He did yesterday!

What I'm saying here is that there's always a relationship between a fresh power and an Old Cloak! The power and anointing a man receive might be novel and pioneering, but then, he must never run into the error of neglecting God's ancient principles. In fact, a man that will last in the anointing must of necessity search out those ancient landmarks and walk in them till they create an unbreakable backbone for him in ministry. If today's Christians walk in a ceaseless flow of the anointing and power, they will constantly kill that porous desire to have something new and different from the unchanging patterns of God from the Old to the New.

To go a long way in the manifestation of what you received at Pentecost, you stay connected to the realities that birth the experience! I want you to see the wisdom of God from the words of Christ Jesus (a man who walked in the fullness of God's power through His earthly ministry). *"Verily, verily, I say unto you, He that believeth on me, the works that I do shall he do also; and greater works than these shall he do; because I go unto my Father."* John 14:12(KJV). Did you see where Jesus said the disciples would begin their work of ministry?

From the works He did! He wanted to create a correct understanding of the connection they have to maintain with Him before they could step into the higher level of manifestation. Even though you will do greater works, you must begin from My works.

You see that you can do more than the great men of Old in your ministry doesn't give you the audacity to cast down the effective orders on which the power of God is built through the ages. No wonder Elijah's last miracle became Elisha's first miracle. Can you imagine that? We saw that Elisha walked with the potency of the Old Cloak (he never threw it into the waste bin of pride) and performed greater works than Elijah. Will you drop your pride like Elisha thorned down his own garment today and pick up the Old Cloak?

Before the fulfillment of Christ Jesus' ministry, we saw Elijah and Moses on the mount of transfiguration to discuss and bring a connection between the law and the prophets into Christ. So, Christ is the encapsulation of the Old and the New orders. He never came to abolish the law but fulfill the same. Hence, what continued in the disciples was an outflow and continuation of what God began in Moses. The works that began in Moses continued in the prophets, culminating in Christ Jesus. Now, Christ Jesus transferred the same baton and cloak to the disciples, and He said, greater works than these will you do. Note, He didn't say, "a different order than this will you establish."

So, today's Christian mandate is not to scatter what God has carefully built but align with it for maximum impact. Members of the body of Christ must carry on the works of Christ while on earth. The disciples were not disobedient to the heavenly vision. The book of Acts became a hallmark for the manifestation of power because certain men walked in close alignment with the Old Cloak their Master handed over to them at Pentecost. The book of Acts revealed that Christ Jesus continued to work through the Apostles in the early church through the instrumentality of the Holy Spirit. Amazingly, the medium of their communication of the truth was purely the Old Testament.

In the gospels, Christ Jesus's works include miracles, but His works also extend to all that He taught and did in obedience to the Father. In John 17:4, Christ Jesus sums up His ministry when He prays, *"I glorified You on the earth, having accomplished the work which You have given Me to do."* So if you are doing the works that Christ Jesus did, and even greater works, it would not only be limited to miracles both also: living in complete dependence on the Father, obeying Him in all things, demonstrating the Father's love and mercy, and confronting the religious errors of our day Christ Jesus did all these things and more.

One clue to the confidence of Christ Jesus that His disciples will do greater works is captured in the phrase *"because I go to the Father."* **Christ Jesus knew that what could connect them with endless power is their awareness of the source of His strength—the Father!** So, when Christ Jesus promised the Holy Spirit, it's to start from where the Father and the Son had just stopped working.

Christ Jesus promised that after He returned to the Father, He would send the Holy Spirit to indwell them. **And so the greater works that the disciples would do were the direct result of the Spirit's working in and through them. Not a result of what they have to do or what they know how to do, purely based on the Spirit of God.** Hence, if a Christian does not remain in Christ and live according to the dictates of the Spirit, he can never manifest God's power accurately because there would be no source from which the power is continuously rekindled! There was a day my wife and i were planning to carry on a ministry's assignment. Jehovah came and asked this "is it a servant to tell a master what he wants to do or the master to tell a servant what to do?"

BUILDING ON CHRIST'S FOUNDATION

However, the Bible reveals that there is a way God does His things that can never be uttered. It's called God's foundation, and the bible describes it thus: *"Nevertheless the foundation of God standeth sure, having this seal, The Lord knoweth them that are his. And, Let every one that nameth the name of Christ depart from iniquity."* 2 Timothy2:19

Can you see the immutability of God's foundation from the scripture above? The potency of all verdicts and sentences is the seal it bears. In ancient times, a king's seal is a representative of him, and in our days, a seal is a symbol of authority and a means of identity. God's ways aren't ambiguous or vague. It has unchanging standards; that is; it has principles and parameters. There are rules in it that can never be changed and laws that can never be ignored. Interestingly, these principles have a seal: there is authorization for it. Just like the scepter of a king, there is a seal that validates the standard of God, and that is: "...*let everyone that nameth the name of Christ depart from iniquity."* Your departure and forsaking of iniquity isn't a matter of choice or debate rather, it is a necessity. If you would have God be by your side at all times, then; you must walk by His standards. And the confirmation that you walk in His standards is that you will depart from iniquity.

The bible says to our faces that *"He that sinneth is of the devil..."* No matter the magnitude of power a man claims to have, if he has not departed from iniquity and has not left the unclean thing, God cannot do much with him because there is a patent of the devil on everything he does. If you try to do the will of God without first forsaking iniquity, you would be scattering and not gathering with the Lord. You cannot be in sin and ask that grace abound. If you will manifest God's power and walk in the miraculous; then, you must first deny every form of ungodliness. **You must come to a place where your life is informed and directed by the Spirit of God and not your**

will because every will a man has outside God can only lead him to disobedience.

To walk in unlimited power as of old, a Christian must be ready to line up with the person of Christ both in character and acts. This is because the summation of God's mandate upon the earth takes its rhapsody in Christ! If the disciples thought it wise to stick with the old rugged way of power and never tried to reinvent the wheel, the Christians of today must know that it's a necessity never to lay a new foundation.

Let's use the relationship between Moses and Joshua as a case study here. After the death of Moses, the servant of God, who walked in the power of God, God introduced to Joshua the scope of what he would do in ministry. God never put down what Moses had done or what He had told Moses because Joshua was about to inherit the Old Cloak of Moses. **God's power never comes to pioneer a different pattern from the Old. But to bring fulfillment and the full-scale manifestation of**

what power there is in the Old. See what God said to Joshua: *"After the death of the LORD's servant Moses,* **the LORD spoke to Moses' helper***, Joshua, son of Nun. He said, "My servant Moses is dead. Get ready now, you and all the people of Israel, and cross the Jordan River into the land that I am giving them.* **As I told Moses***, I have given you and all my people the entire land that you will be marching over. Your borders will reach from the desert in the south to the Lebanon Mountains in the north; from the great Euphrates River in the east, through the Hittite country, to the Mediterranean Sea in the west. Joshua, no one will be able to defeat you as long as you live.* **I will be with you as I was with Moses***. I will always be with you; I will never abandon you."*
Joshua 1:1-5

Wow! Did you see God constantly making reference to the order He already established with Moses? God was going to anoint Joshua for the battle, but Joshua must be trained to know how to handle the fresh anointing with the already established heavenly protocols. **In**

the school of the spirit, you don't do what you like. You relate with an Immortal King. Hence, His counsels are eternal! God told Joshua the same thing He already told Moses.

You see, if the Christians of today will come into the power as of old, there's a need for a critical examination of our neglect of the Old Cloak. We see a reoccurring pattern of this connection between the new and the Old Cloak expressed in a wider scope in the experience of Moses and Joshua—his disciple. Remember I said God constantly brought Joshua into the realities of His promise to Joshua for effectiveness in ministry. **Now, after Joshua received the cloak of Power, he came into the same level of experience and dominion Moses**—his master had as a servant of God.

Moses took off his sandals in Exodus 3:5 as a symbol of absolute surrender in stepping into the power of God. And amazingly, Joshua had to take off his sandals too in the book of Joshua 5:15 in surrender to the lord of host before he could conquer without restraints. Because of this similar order of encounters, a connection was fostered that birth a similar manifestation of God's power in Joshua's leadership.

For instance, when Moses led the people of Israel out of the land of bondage, he parted the red sea by the power of God to establish the freedom of God's people. Also, when God called Joshua, he was able to walk in the same expression of God's power by parting River Jordan to grant the people of God access into their rest.

The point is, if Joshua must succeed in ministry, he must step back in time to see the wealth of realities kept in his father for him to journey correctly. *Joshua* of today—Christians—must never despise what God used great men in the scriptures to establish as solid foundation for inheriting God's power. Don't build your Christian life on a miry clay of new inventions of cloaks and patterns! There's one God has made firm and solid—Christ Jesus. Line up with HIM!

DOING GREATER WORKS THAN CHRIST BUT NOT DIFFERENT THINGS

Having learned the importance of standing in Christ and building on His foundation, it is sacrosanct to understand that you have been ordained to do greater things in Christ but not different things from Him. Christ never gave the believer a mandate to do different things than He did; He only said: 'Greater works than this…' (John 14:12 KJV). The believer is meant to access the Father through Jesus's name for the performance and activation of these promises. In John 14:13-14 (NKJV): the bible says that *Whatever you ask in my name, that will I do, so that the Father may be glorified in the Son. If you ask me anything in my name, I will do it."* In these verses, we see the extent, the basis, the objective, and the result of Jesus' promise:

THE EXTENT OF JESUS' PROMISE: "WHATEVER YOU ASK."

The context of "whatever you ask" is tied into doing Christ Jesus' works, not seeking your own wills and comforts. John Piper argues that instead of using prayer as a wartime walkie-talkie to call in supplies for the battle, we have turned it into an intercom to ask for more comforts in the den (Let the Nations be Glad ([Baker Academic], p. 49). But prayer isn't a means of getting God to give us what we want so that our lives can be comfier. Rather, prayer is the means by which we ask God to extend His kingdom and do His will on earth as it is in heaven (Matt. 6:10). True, there is a place to ask God to meet our needs. But the center of all that we pray should be, "Lord, do your work through your people! Bring sinners to genuine conversion! Sanctify your people so that we will be faithful representatives of Christ Jesus on earth!"

• THE BASIS OF CHRIST JESUS' PROMISE: "IN MY NAME."

While we must be obedient to Christ if we expect Him to answer our prayers (John 14:15), we don't ask on the basis of our obedience: "I've been really good, so you need to answer this!" Rather, to ask in Jesus' name means that you come to the Father through the Son as your High Priest. To ask in Jesus' name is to recognize that His name is above every name that is named, both in this age and in the age to come (Eph. 1:21). He has the power to answer!

- **THE OBJECTIVE OF CHRIST JESUS' PROMISE: THE FATHER'S GLORY IN THE SON.**

This is a further condition that must govern the *"whatever"* we ask: Our desire is to see God glorified through the Lord Jesus. This may include the salvation of a loved one or of an enemy of the gospel (such as Paul before his conversion). This extends to praying for the gospel to penetrate unreached peoples around the world. It includes praying that troubled marriages may be healed. The main objective is not that they would be happy (although they

91

will), but that God would be glorified through Christ being seen in that marriage. God's glory is the main objective of our prayers.

- **THE RESULT OF JESUS' PROMISE: "I WILL DO IT."**

The result of our praying should be that Christ Jesus does it. This implies Christ's deity: He has the power to answer whatever we ask. But this is where it gets difficult because many of our prayers would seemingly further God's kingdom and glory, but He has not done it. So, how do we reconcile Christ Jesus' seeming blanket promise to answer prayers in His name for God's glory with the fact that many such prayers go unanswered? You must learn to hold on to commit yourself to the cause of Christ, not yours!

CHAPTER SIX

EFFECTS OF THE PORTION; POWER IN TODAY'S CHURCH

In every race, there are participants who contend for the prize, and the length of the race will determine the level of strength an athlete will need. If it's a 100-meter sprint or 100-meter hurdle, the major qualification for getting the prize will be speed and agility. So, in a sprint, let's say a 100-meter race, immediately the gun is shot; sprinters will immediately take-off from their starting blocks and continue increasing in speed. In other words, athletes in a 100-meter sprint compete based on speed. Hence, the race is always short and can be finished in as fast as 9.80 seconds.

However, in long-distance races, an athlete will need more than speed and agility; he will need power, endurance, and strength. The longer the race, the lesser speed matters. In most marathons, after the gun is shot to start the race, athletes start at a very slow speed because they understand that they are going a long way, and speed will wear them out on time. What they need is power, strength, and endurance, not speed.

As Christians, God has not called us to just flash through the earth like a strand of lightning. Rather, we are saved to be a shining light on earth and an epitome of God's power and eternal make-up. We're here to help the world see His marvelous light and submit to His grace. Paul talks about this in the book of Hebrews 12: 1, when he says, *"Wherefore seeing we also are compassed about with so great a cloud of witnesses, let us lay aside every weight, and the sin which doth so easily beset us, and let us run with patience the race that is set before us."* (KJV)

He mentions in the scripture quotation above that we should run with patience, the race that is set before us. This is a pointer to the fact that Christians have been called to a marathon and not a sprint. Only a long race requires patience and techniques. Hence if you as a Christian will go far in life and in ministry, it's not speeding or immediate results you need; it's God's power, strength, and agility.

We cannot overemphasize how much the Christian of today needs God's power to frontier God's work here on earth. To move God's work forward in this stormy world, you do not just need brilliance, intelligence, or physical energies to do so. You need something deeper than wonderful and well-arranged talk to deliver the world from darkness. Imagine Elisha before river Jordan without the Old Cloak of power. **You see, river Jordan will not bow to your degree. It only bows to the man that is endued with power from on high.**

Sweet talks and excellent exegesis of scriptures with no touch with the essence of power are merely a carnal exercise! Elisha didn't go back to the river to beg it to part as it did before Elijah. No! There was something in Elisha's hands now capable of the parting river Jordan—the Old Cloak of power he received from Elijah. Elisha would have remained stranded on the other side of the river if not for the effect of the portion he received and the Old Cloak.

No wonder the bible revealed that *"Say unto God, How terrible art thou in thy works! through the greatness of thy power shall thine enemies submit themselves unto thee."* Psalm 66:3. Wow! The enemy of the church, your family, and children will not submit because you finished from Harvard or Oxford University. They submit by the effulgence of God's power! Spiritual battles cannot be fought on the energies of the flesh. **You must be endued with power to live the Christian life accurately.**

Hence, just like Elisha picked up the Old Cloak and worked the exact miracles his master worked, the Christian of today must align with the outpouring of the Spirit to function in the fullness of God's power. Elijah doesn't only express power; he exercised dominion the same way his master exercised it. There was no break in the move of God's ever-increasing power in Elisha's lifetime. In this chapter, I will bring you into the importance and expression of God's power in the church of today so that we may come into the avalanche of God's eternal resources.

GOD'S POWER AND THE CHURCH TODAY

"And he said unto them, it is not for you to know the times or the seasons, which the Father hath put in his own power. But ye shall receive power, after that the Holy Ghost is come upon you: and ye shall be witnesses unto me both in Jerusalem, and in all Judaea, and in Samaria, and unto the uttermost part of the earth."

- Acts 1:7-8 (KJV)

Let me quickly let you in on what's going on right there in the book of Acts. That was Christ Jesus' instruction to the disciples before they take off like a tornado. Christ Jesus knew that the disciples weren't set for the ministry before them until they are filled with power. The paddle of power was a key factor in stepping into the ocean of kingdom advancement. Without it, they have no spiritual backing as a true witness of Christ. The same thing applies to the church today. Without the outpouring of God's power on the church afresh as of Old, the mandate of dominion is never going to be possible.

The church does not necessarily denote a building where Christian worship takes place, but it is the whole body of Christians. John V. Newman puts it this way: "the one church is the whole body gathered together from all ages." Hence, when we refer to the church of God, it is not a denomination or a particular person we are talking about but the general body of believers that are around at a particular dispensation.

When Christ left the earth, He gave commandment to the church as to how they should live and what they are expected to do. Just like a manager going to a larger branch gives duty with specific job descriptions to his employees. Christ gave His disciples the duty of occupying till He comes in Luke 19:13 with the specific job description spelled out vividly in Matthew 28: 19-20: *"Go ye therefore, and teach all nations, baptizing them in the name of the Father, and of the Son, and of the Holy*

Ghost: Teaching them to observe all things whatsoever I have commanded you: and, lo, I am with you alway, even unto the end of the world. Amen." **With such a great task ahead of it, the church will surely need more than just willpower and obedience. It will need constant interaction with God's power!**

Hence, the bible says in Acts 1:7-8 that you shall receive power after the Holy Ghost comes upon you. The power of God will be ushered in by the introduction of a new person into the Christian life: the Holy Spirit. God's power was released for witnessing and empowerment when the Holy Spirit was released on the eventful day of Pentecost. It was just like Elisha picking up his master's cloak with the fullness of assurance to go and establish dominion.

You must understand that there's a difference between the working of God's Spirit within a Christian and His outpouring upon them. When you gave your life to Christ, the Holy Spirit comes within you, but its manifestations are not fully activated. This is the essence of another spiritual experience called: 'the Holy Ghost Baptism.' This was what happened in Acts 2 when the Spirit of God rested on Christians who already had God's Spirit in them for the activation of a different and dynamic spiritual operation.

This is the power Christians need in the Church today: the power that came at Pentecost. The Church must understand that theological knowledge and activities in living the Christian life are never enough. **Power is the only effectual thing through which the Christian life can be maximally lived**. Remember, you have been called to a marathon journey and not a sprint. You need more than speed; accuracy and agility will even prove insufficient: what will see you through is power. You see, power is not just an ability but a spirit-powered capability. While ability is a quality or state of being able, capability is the facility or faculty capable of development. Power is not only something you have (ability) but a possession of yours that can be developed (capability).

If the prophets of Old couldn't move God's agenda forward in their generation, and the early church rose mightily on the wings of power, what makes you think you can be a Christian today and be effective without power? The disciples how helpless they were without the availability of God's unending ability constantly supplied. Two critical tools they employed in rekindling the flame of God's power in their Christian life were waiting in prayer and the word of God. When these two powerful tools mix adequately in the church, we enter a season of endless manifestation of God's power.

It was in the book of James that we saw the strength of Elijah's power to shut the windows of heaven for three years. It wasn't empty talk before Ahab. It was an utterance powered by the constant prayer posture he sustained before God. For the church to walk in the effulgence of the same power, we must subscribe to the ministry of prayer. **Remember, demons don't go out by advice. They go out by the finger of God—power of God!**

The church is fashioned to interact with power consistently. Why? It was established and built by men clothed with the same. You don't conquer kingdoms without power. So, the uttermost part of the earth will only be worth taking after the church is baptized with power as of Old. We have become so educated in our days that we lack simple faith in the power of God. Peter, a fisherman, walked in such a deep dimension of God's power that his shadow began to heal the sick. This was how important power was to the Apostles of Old.

Amazingly, even though they walked in such dimensions of power, they never get relaxed and puffed up by pride to go in search of another cloak of power. The power they received could sustain the church through every thick and thin without any loss. They were walking in the same realities Christ Jesus walked in (and even more) because they took up His Old Cloak on the day of Pentecost. Elijah's cloak parted River Jordan, Christ Jesus' gift of the Holy Spirit, drew five thousand men into the kingdom. The same Cloak! The same order! The same result!

EFFICACY OF POWER IN THE CHURCH TODAY

Having seen the importance of power in the church today, it is important you understand specific things the power of God can help you achieve in your Christian journey. You've got to know exactly how God's power will help you in your race.

First, it affords you the strength to do God's will perpetually. Once God's Spirit empowers you, it becomes easy for you to know God's will and do it without fear or restraint. The bible puts it thus in Philippians 2:13: *"For it is God which worketh in you both to will and to do of his good pleasure."* Did you see that it's God that empowers you to think the way He thinks and to see things the way He does? **When the power of God is poured out on the believer, he becomes defiant and passionate at doing whatever brings glory to God.**

Hence, the effect of God's power is to make Christians think and act like God.

Also, **God's power paves the way for dominion and supremacy over sin, self, and the world.** In Matthew 9:6, Christ emphasizes this power by saying: *"But that ye may know that the Son of man hath power on earth to forgive sins, (then saith he to the sick of the palsy,) Arise, take up thy bed, and go unto thine house."* If Christ's power could forgive sin, it could also make the sinner free from the life of sin.

Hence, Christians are no longer under the power and shackles of sin and self but under the power of God, who has redeemed them. That isn't the only thing that God's power does. In 2 Peter 1:3; the bible says that *"According as his divine power hath given unto us all things that pertain unto life and godliness, through the knowledge of him that hath called us to glory and virtue:"* His power has created a background for you to access all the possibilities available for you in Christ. The absence of power will only lead to a reduced potency in expressing God's life.

Every believer is granted access to the miraculous by the power of God given to them. **Salvation brings every believer to the realm of no limitation, and everything available in Christ becomes available to them**. But when a believer does not know the efficacy of the power he has received, he will live like a man helpless and beggarly. It's just like someone who has a blank check to fill for any of His needs but still keeps on allowing in abject poverty and excessive needs. This is the pitiable state of the church today.

Finally, God's power empowers you as a Christian for soul-winning. It helps you to bear fruits as Christ did. The book of Acts quoted above says that *"...you shall be witnesses to me in Jerusalem, in Judaea and to the uttermost parts of the earth."* After the power of God rests on a Christian, He equips and empowers him for active soul-winning. This power doesn't only give boldness and courage but also allows Christians to perform miracles like

Christ and even more for the salvation of souls and glorification of God's name.

All through the ages, men and women have followed Christ patiently till this power was activated in their lives, and the church today is still reaping the benefits of what the power they received achieved. People like: William J. Seymour, John G. Lake, Kathryn Kuhlman, and Aimee Semple McPherson were ordinary men and women who only followed God with resolve and a desire to see His power flow in their lives and generation. We can see the effects God's power has had on their lives and ministries and how even after their deaths, they continue to affects lives and destinies. This kind of expression and manifestation of power is what the church needs in this generation, but we will never get there until we learn to wait on God and follow Him through standing on His standards and principles.

CHAPTER SEVEN

KEEP THE OLD CLOAK; THE PORTION IS YOURS

Steven Torres and his dad loved to have fun. They often played cards, kickball, and hide and seek together. Sadly, those good times came to an abrupt end when Steven's dad died. "Unfortunately, God took him at the age of 38 due to cancer. It felt like Steve were losing everything."

Steven grew up in church and begged God for an answer about why his dad died. He felt he never got one and thought God had abandoned him. "I think my logic was, 'I'm pushing you away. I'm going to do this on my terms.'"

Then, from his teen years through college, he lived for the next party. "I was going to hang out with my friends or my fraternity brothers or the drinking, and the numerous relationships with females. I felt like I was on top of the world. Even though I had all these people, all these associations, all these girls, I felt alone."

At age 37, something happened that shook his world. "They found a tumor, lump, you know, and that it was cancerous. It was, ironically, almost the same age as my father, and that was like the red flag that came into my life, and I was very scared. I reached out to God and said, 'Please, don't do this right now. I don't want my kids to grow up without a father.'"

Steven went through treatments for cancer, and the tumors shrunk. Once the cancer was gone, he stopped praying. "I felt like God didn't answer me the first time. I felt like 'this is all my doing. I've got this under control. Got my treatment, follow what the doctor says to do.' Again, with my logic, 'it's going to be on my terms.'"

The cancer returned four months later. Steven was confident he could beat it, "I didn't have much fear, you know. It ended up going for another six months of treatment, radiation, and chemo. They said they had gotten everything."

After a few months, the cancer returned yet again. By now, Steven was tired and scared. The cancer had metastasized to his stomach and was becoming more aggressive. "I was like 'This can't be'; overwhelming. I started bawling, crying, very upset," he said.

Steven saw on Facebook that a girl he knew from the 4th grade, Shawn, had posted scripture. "I started to read and edit, and within an hour, I started to feel very at ease and comfortable and peaceful. And it was almost like a light switch went off in me that. That void, that thing that I was missing, was always there all along, and that it was God. He had been reaching out, talking to me, and trying to get my attention."

A few days later, Shawn sent Steven an encouraging message. "'God's going to take that cancer, and He's going to crumble it up like a piece of paper and throw it away into the dumpster.'" The next Sunday, Steven made a decision. For the first time in years, he attended church. "I remember the pastor praying. As he was praying and talking, it wasn't his voice I was hearing. To me, I felt like it was God speaking. I knew then that everything I had in my heart and soul was all to God."

Three days later, Steven heard the best news of his life. "They had done some blood work. There was nothing, nothing in my body. And I started crying like a little kid, knowing that, 'wow, He took that out of me.'" To date, Steven has stayed in Christ's love, and his cancer has never ever returned: It's gone forever!

You see, when God blesses man with His divine presence and power, it is the greatest privilege a man can enjoy from God. **Hence, it takes active engagement and deliberate living to maintain whatever it is you have received from God. God is not a swine who inhabits any provided environment.** He is the

Lord of the whole universe, the Holy lone, who is very selective about His environments. He can never dwell in darkness, and this is why this book has introduced you earlier to how you can encounter God's light and be effective with it. However, in this chapter, you will be exposed to things you have to take cognizance of that you might be able to maintain, keep and retain God's power.

Defile not therefore the land which ye shall inhabit, wherein I dwell: for I the Lord dwell among the children of Israel. Numbers 35:34 KJV.

Then her former husband, who sent her away, may not take her again to be his wife, after she has been defiled, for that is an abomination before the Lord. And you shall not bring sin upon the land that the Lord your God is giving you for an inheritance. Deuteronomy 24:4 ESV.

STEPS TO TAKE IN RETAINING THE POWER OF GOD

In the story above, Stephen was just a boy who loved his father like every other young boy. When his father died, and he couldn't understand why it had to happen, he sought an explanation from God but didn't receive anything. This is not because God is cruel, but it is meant to work patience and trust in Him. **The first things you must learn in maintaining God's power and presence are patience and persistence.**

You must understand that patience is not just the ability to wait but the action(s) you are engaged in while waiting. If while waiting, you murmur and complain: you are not waiting; you are only stuck! Persistence, on the other hand, is to persevere and invest continued effort into achieving something. There are times when you will pray for a manifestation of God's power or Spiritual gift, and you won't see the realization of it. This is not happening because you do not have enough access to

God's power, but it might be because God wants to teach you patience and persistence.

In the same vein, Stephen left God as a way of seeking answers, and he never really found them till he came back to God. Another way to retain God's power is to understand that He is the source of it and that power will not thrive without good, consistent fellowship with him. You cannot fellowship with mammon and expect God to express Himself through you. **A man can only carry the aura of an environment he tarries in.** If you would have God's power continuously revealed in you and through you, then you must continue steadfastly in studying His words and seeking His face through prayer. There was a day Jehovah told me that there is a category of Christian Believers who are after solutions instead of relationship with Him and that this category easily turns itself as prey to the world and to the devil.

You see, the power you have inherited from God is such a great one that nothing in heaven and on earth can be compared to it. It is God's divine power manifested in you! But then, people around you will say many things about you and the life you now live. In the story of Elisha and Elijah in 2Kimgs2, the sons of the prophets continued mocking Elisha till the power was revealed in Him. Most times, it won't be only unbelievers that will mock you but Christians and even pastors. It is your duty then to hold on to God in Faith and know whom you have believed. Paul went through this same situation, rulers stood against him, pagans stood against him, Christians stood against him, and even his own disciples forsook him, but he held on to who he had believed through faith, and he could say:

"Who shall separate us from the love of Christ? Shall tribulation, or distress, or persecution, or famine, or nakedness, or peril, or sword? For I am persuaded, that neither death, nor life, nor angels, nor principalities, nor powers, nor things present, nor things to come, Nor height, nor depth, nor any other creature, shall be able to separate us from the

love of God, which is in Christ Jesus our Lord."

- Romans 8:35,38-39(KJV)

The way to maintaining God's power is to get to a level where nothing or no one can separate you from His love nor stand between you and His love. God's power can adequately be manifested through the life of men when they are submissive to Him and to His love. He is not looking for a co-pilot to steer the course of His plans in you. No! Instead, He is looking for a submissive vessel that He will navigate through the storms and turmoil till it gets to the land of unending bliss.

In the story of Stephen above, his cancer continued coming back, and his healing was not permanent because he wasn't fully submitted to God. The glory due to God, he shared it between himself and the doctor. This is the disheartening state of the church today! Pastors are too prominent on their pulpits that God is no longer seen, sermons are too well-planned and strategically crafted that there is no provision for God's inspiration and message till the church comes to a place where God is the administrator of all! God's power will only visit the church for a while and then leave like it never came.

Beloved, there was a time the Most High asked me who was behind the speed the congregations are built? Then on another occasion, He showed me how people were filling the churches, but praises were instead going to leaders. We honestly do a lot in the name of Christ but, with our mind because we are naturally hard-working individuals but the ability and the power to wait for direction is what we lack because it is not natural, and it is difficult to submit the flesh and its zeal under the control of the Holy Spirit and the perfect will of Yahweh.

RETAINING GOD'S POWER THROUGH FAITH

"But without faith, *it is* impossible to please *him:* for he that cometh to God must believe that he is and *that* he is a rewarder of them that diligently seek him."

- Hebrews 11:6(KJV)

Faith, according to the first verse of Hebrews 11, is the substance of things hoped for and assurance of things not seen. According to Merriam-Webster's dictionary, a substance is a physical material from which something is made or which has discrete existence. Faith being a substance means it is not an abstract representation of an arbitrary phenomenon, but rather, faith is tangible. It's a physical expression that can be observed. By being an assurance, faith is holding on to what is not physically present with clear visibility. It isn't here, but you can see it clearly.

This is the most essential element of walking with God and retaining His power and presence. The bible says in the scripture quoted above that without faith, it is impossible to please God. **There is nothing you do in God without faith that is acceptable.** As a matter of fact, when you give anything to God without faith, it does not please Him. **Faith is the currency through which God's trust and assent are obtained**.

Hence, if you would maintain God's power and presence, you must have faith in Him. You must hold His words as through and never changing; He cannot lie! In your practice of faith, you don't just believe God can do it; you know He has done it. A group of Christians once prayed with a sick brother, and after praying, there was no manifestation of his healing. So one brother asked them all, who will continue praying that our brother may be healed after leaving here? Almost everyone raised their hands, and he asks: "what for?" They all stood in silence-

"I personally believe that God has healed Him, and I will not pray that he be healed again; I will only pray that God brings the physical manifestation of what He had perfected." Did you see that? Such expressions of faith can make us express deeper dynamics of God's miracles and scale higher altitudes in His grace.

Having read through the pages of this book, it will be critical for you to run a check on your heart to know if you're still stuck in the belief that the New came to take away the Ancient principles of God's word. Are you still on the verge of contemplation that today's Christians have nothing to do with the law—especially the happenings of the Old Testament—taking Pentecost and the Holy Spirit's permanent residence in such a Christian as the reason? I suppose not. Patiently align with the wealth of God's power hidden in the pages of the Old Testament to find your way through the depth of the New Testament.

Conclusion

Despite attempts by today's crop of Christians--clergy especially-- to malign the Old Testament, or redefine its value to the New Testament Christian, God's Holy Spirit conflicts with them and gives the grace to reveal such errors to Christians through this kind of book.

If times and seasons--present-day civilization-- has made some Christians believe in this false narrative, be confident that there are solace and safety in knowing that even Christ--whom they claim to obey-- quoted letters from the Old Testament whenever He said, "it is written."

And while they seem to cut out the acts of the fathers of old, what matters is that they're on the other side of truth, and you now know that.

Besides, any set of believers or supposed Christians who believe in the false narrative of the uselessness of the Old Testament should be queried if they have God's Spirit. Because the Spirit who worked in the days of old doesn't deny His active involvement in these days of the New Covenant, but according to 2 Corinthians 11:4, *"For if he that cometh preacheth another Jesus, whom we have not preached, or if ye receive another spirit, which ye have not received, or another gospel, which ye have not accepted, ye might well bear with him."*

However, there's no argument about the only way to fellowship with God--through Christ Jesus alone. Yet, today's church seems to lack His evident power. More so, the place of fervent, spirit-led discipleship seems to be replaced with praise-singing and glory-seeking gimmicks. More so, in today's church, many seem to curry the favor of those who are deemed, spiritual leaders. While this is not only against Christ's design for greatness--that aspiring masters must serve their followers instead-- many in today's church appear not to bat an eyelid in this utter rebellion.

Hence, what can be said about these people? Flee! Be careful and don't give them a listening ear if they persist with such behaviors and heresies!! This may be a telling reason for the absence of God's Spirit and power in many congregations. Paul further explains in 2 Timothy 4:3-4, *"For the time will come when they will not endure sound doctrine; but after their own lusts shall they heap to themselves teachers, having itching ears; And they shall turn away their ears from the truth, and shall be turned unto fables."*

So, today's church, unlike the old, seems to replace sound and wholesome teachings with mere speeches or fables masked with eloquence and behind such masks, error and heresy. Unfortunately, due to ignorance about proper discipleship, many have become semi-idolaters; they rather seek the approval and score of their preachers--more bewildering is how much they give full support to such leaders, even if heretic and erroneous.

Hence, the place of intimacy with God and the seeking of Christ's pleasure as a template for true discipleship are put aside. They seem to neglect the indwelling Spirit or the knowledge of His word for the preacher's opinion and remarks. It indeed appears that many will rather jettison the inheritance of being the friends of God for being friends with pastors who misleads them.

Whereas, had today's Christians subjected to thorough learning according to 2 Timothy 2:15, *"Study to shew thyself approved unto God, a workman that needeth not to be ashamed, rightly dividing the word of truth."* they wouldn't miss out on the benefits of the lessons of the Old Testament that was written for the Christian's example and learning. But that Old Cloak, though it seems ragged, unattractive, and rough, is the template to understand true discipleship during these perilous times and seasons.

Is God's will fulfilled when the church doesn't cling to the Old Cloak? The scriptures say in Hebrews 13:8, *"Jesus Christ the same yesterday, and today, and forever."* Similarly, discipleship can't be properly forged or baked without exploring the Old Cloak. Isn't it high time that today's church redefined its assessment, judgment, and understanding of God's will?

Though this can't be done through human strength, God's will should be carried out and facilitated by His Spirit in every Christians today. As Elisha received the double portion, shouldn't today's Christians likewise cling to the grace supplied by God's Spirit to tackle lack of power, love, presence, soberness, and their lack of discipline; lack of fear for Jehovah; and perhaps an excessive focus on bread?

Expressly, our topic--the Old Cloak-- aims to quicken today's church by means of remembrance. So be renewed in your mind, and feel free to thrust into the Old and New Testament alike for more of Christ's bounties. As 2 Timothy 3:16-17 says, *"All scripture is given by inspiration of God, and is profitable for doctrine, for reproof, for correction, for instruction in righteousness: That the man of*

God may be perfect, thoroughly furnished unto all good works. "

The above is a New Testament passage that conjoins the importance of the Old Testament-- all scriptures-- with its beneficial prowess to today's Christian--the man of God. Hence, don't believe otherwise, but cling to the Old Cloak and be blessed.

By God's grace, a firm, steady hold on the Old Cloak should shed all forms of lukewarmness, stagnation, and carelessness in today's Church. Therefore, the best advice you'd probably get as a Christian in today's world is to secure and understand God's ways via the Old Testament, with its accompanying New Testament implications. Cling to the Old Cloak--His ways of power, presence, and glory-- with the Holy Spirit's role as a teacher helping you all the way! Amen.

OTHER BOOKS FROM THE SAME AUTHORS

1. The Original Plan of God For Marriage

2. Personal Deliverance Ministry

3. The Road To Heaven

4. Understanding The Mystery & Power Of A Living Faith

5. The Followers Of Jesus Christ In The School Of Life: Part 1, 2, 3 and 4

6. The Heart Beat And The Word Of Prophecy

7. The Followers Of Jesus Christ In The School Of Life: Part V – The School Of Prayer

8. The Most Controversial Name of All Times: The Messiah.

9. The Foundation Of A Born Again Christian

10. Christian Living: Temptation